j. t. baka

holocene

one double album of lyrics

LIGHTness

alluvium

old lady biplane

badly hit

stumbled and tumbled

from cloud to cloud

until diving out of control

catching herself just about sea level

limbing from wave to wave

praying

the engine

might last long enough

until reaching the coast

and really

the coast was not far off

the coastline already in sight

but then

a simple gust of wind

punched all life

out of her

impaling herself

on a rock

not very far from the shore

she did

wave after wave

crushing against the rock

wave after wave

smashing her against the rock

wave after wave

smashing and crushing her

into a trillion pieces

wave after wave

taking the pieces with it

on its journey to the shore

wave after wave

crushing against the shore

hurling the broken pieces

of what was once her

a beauty of a bird

on the beach

spilling her splattered insides

all over the place

for everyone to see

what an old biplane

is capable of to endure

before surrender

and for everyone to see

what the wrath of the sea

is capable of

at the end of the demonstration

in her mercy

the sea is even giving free the pilot

washing up

on the beach

broken

and cut open like a fish

splattered insides

offering deep insights

of how much man is able of suffering

the despair of blindness

the corona

of the saviour

sending its rays

into the hollowed hearts

of the despaired

injecting the vaccine of love

poisoning what's left

of a future past

of what wasn't

the end of history

but just another fool's pyrrhic victory

the cat is

always chasing

its own tail

the blindness of despair

the despaired

the despair of love

the love of despair

the despair of empathy

the empathy of despair

the despair of shallowness

the shallowness of despair

the despair of emptiness

the emptiness of despair

the despair of loniless

the loniless of despair

the despair of life

a life of despair

on the edge

flying high above the dessert

near the ice barrier

I saw a duck walking along the ice

just by itself

what was it doing

right here

on the edge of the world

at this time of day

carefully treating

its way

it just looked like me

when I

back in the day

was walking along the strand

looking for making a grand

without having to make a last stand

I felt for

this cute little creature

this fellow traveller

this brother in arms

this comrade of compassion

waddling its way

up the ice

my heart was about to break

tears were streaming

down my cheeks

while I was taking my gun

loading

unlocking

aiming

and then taking a deep breath

I could taste

the salt of my tears

the endless depths of melancholy

I was about to lose

myself into

to save the koala from the wall of fire

it was about to climb right into

it took

one shot

high above the desert

all it took

was just one shot

to save me

a child

living in the cold emptiness

of a shallow love

existing in a frozen void

of superficial empathy

breathing in the sterile nihilism

of a childless mother

growing into fossilized memories

of a nostalgic melancholy

living the undead life

of important things

left undone

and then forgotten

aborted

obituary

look

at these hands

once

they were slim

the fingers long and elegant

likes the ones

of piano players and models

now

they are broad and thick

the fingers gnarled

the texture of the skin rough

but still

despite of old age

they write well

the despair of the future

what's next

the future of despair

who's next

but don't let us wax

nostalgic about the future

as we knew it

let us umbrace the new tried

and true apocalyptic vision of it

WHOOOOOSH

WAVES

[bridge]

looking at

how they look at you

staring actually

looking at

how they stare at you

at your beauty

you show them

all of your beauty

you show off

on the catwalk

because that's

what you are

indulging in their stares

at you

you enjoy living

until

there is only their stares

through which you live

until

all you see

is how

they look at you

until

all you see

is the way

they look at you

until

you see yourself

the way

they see you

until

you see yourself

how the bully did

back then

all you

see

all there

is

is

what he

saw what they

see

and they

are right

you have to work

harder

you have to eat

even less

until

there is only

this feeling

that eats

you up

not the scale

of the weight

not their stares

the hunger

for less

until

there is

only hunger for more

but

luckily

there is your friend

and

your friend helps you

fighting

all the hunger in the world

without gaining weight

until

all you want

is more

of your friend

one more

pill

one more

sniff

one more

shot

to keep you awake

to keep you going

to keep you alive

to keep you in this world

of stares

to keep you

until

it's eating you out

until

it is the only thing

you hunger for

until

it is the only thing

there is

until

it is the only thing

that keeps you human

if you have it

until

it doesn't

because

it didn't eat just your personality

and your very soul

the one you already sold

no

it was eating everything

and what

can you do

without your looks

without your beauty

at first though

no biggie

just not the best jobs

out there

and who wants to be

the best paid whore

anyway

until

the not so well-paid blow jobs

are totally out of reach

too

and what

once

looked like

a fight for

this or that kind of car

bringing you to the blow job

is suddenly

no car at all

and is suddenly

nothing at all

only the stare of the bully again

because

again you are nothing

with no money

for friends

with no money

for rent

with no money

for food even

with nothing

but fear

the all-consuming fear

for your very own existence

for your life

not even love

can help you

you already

lost it

somewhere in between

but you

still fussing over it

and you hold onto it

it is the only thing left

the only thing
that's there for you

keeping you warm and cozy
in the cold outside

nobody can take it
from you

nobody wants to take it
from you

it is all yours

because it's already gone

it is safe and

unreal

like the sickness

was unreal at first

until the pain

started to come in waves

rolling all over you

sinking and burying you

under its monster waves

taking everything

with them

leaving nothing behind but pain

but not the nice pain

of a love lost

a much different pain

than you were used to

a different pain

from the ones

you tried to kill

every time

with another pain

a pain with the intention

to stay

for good

a pain full of mercy

because it is not personal actually

it is not interested in you

as a person like the bully

it doesn't want to make you

UGLY

it doesn't want to take your soul

just your life

a pain

so different and difficult and yet

so simple

but again

so all-consuming

in its own way

taking away everything

you already thought lost

again

looks

fun

love

even your dignity

erasing you

bit by bit

until you are gone

for good

with some things

it is funny

as you already know

some things are true

until there are not any more

until they are true again

like written words

and words you write

they can come to you

and fill you up

they have the power

to build

love

new life

better futures

brighter worlds

happiness

the power of

imagination

until

there is nothing else

but these very words

in which

what is left of you

believes

a vision of a world

different

a vision of an end

different

hope

until

a new shock wave

arrives and is drowning everything out

in an deep blue primeval roar of pain

until

the catfish's rising

meet me

on the shore

darkNESS

alluvium

because there was

nothing else to do

the wind started to follow

the movement of this most peculiar bird

made from wood and canvas

the bird's movements

were erratic

and sometimes

it looked like

the bird was about to loose

balance and control

completely

and was about to fall

in oblivion

so the wind

decided to help

his new friend

and pushed her up

badly hit

the bird

was fighting for her life

she stumbled

from cloud to cloud

praying

the engine might last

until reaching the coast at least

and indeed

the coast was not

far off

the coastline already in sight

by then

the wind had lost all interest already

bored

the wind gave her

one last push

punching out all lights

knocking her right out of the sky

spiraling

out of control

completely

racing

head over heels

straight down to earth

impaling herself

on a rock

not too far from the shore

because there was

nothing else to do

the sea fell in love

with this peculiar creature

wrapped around the rock

sending out waves

the sea tried to establish

communications

wave after wave

crushing against the rock

wave after wave

crushing into the creature

wave after wave

grinding it

into a zillion pieces

wave after wave

taking them with it

on its journey to the shore

showing them around

trying to arouse their interest

in the blue world of wonders around them

but by reaching the shore

the sea lost all interest

bored

hurling the pieces of the creature

wave after wave

on the beach

with the fury of a betrayed lover

for everyone to see

what the sea's might is capable of if

at the very last

the sea was even giving up

on the creatue inside the creature

a creature even more

interesting and marvelous

than the other one

washing up on the shore

broken and cut open

like a fish

splattered insides

offering deep insights

of how much man

was capable of suffering

for friendship and love

and a future

executed

humor

if it's not happening

for the first time

it's like going

through the motions

although

of course

it confronts you

with not so small a problem

to lose your job

in the age of corona

if it's not happening

for the first time

it's like going through

the motions

although

of course

it causes your world

to collapse

to lose everything

you hold dear

when the love of your life

breaks up with you

in time with corona

if it happened not once

but twice

to see a person

you are related to

succumbing to cancer

you are at least

warned

although

of course

dying of cancer

is not as easy as it looks

but as you know

atomic sunsets

will be the most romantic thing

you are ever going to see

and if it's not happening

for the first time

it is like going through the motions

cat's avenue

I see me

on a cold morning

walking along cat's avenue

early morning

too early for the sun to show up

hiding behind a vail of clouds

too early

for the inhabitants

of this part of the city

to populate the sidewalks

or

are they just hiding from me

I wonder

but with the sun

showing her face

bit by bit

ray by ray

but with the temperature

rising

notch by notch

degree by degree

I see

tails turning up

the pointed tips of ears

rising out of nowhere

I hear flurry steps in a hurry

hushed panting

cat calls in the distance

finally

they show themselves

proud and arrogant

completely disinterested

in this new face

at first

but step by step

their attitude changes

turning their faces

towards me

they start to follow me

coming closer and closer

they start to smile

to reach out to me

closing in

they grab me

tossing me in the air

and then carrying me

on their shoulders

celebrating me

like a hero of old

coming home from battle

victorious

but suddenly

I find myself in an alley

with a dead end

alone

looking up

all I can see

are dark clouds

open up

pouring cold rain

down on me

seeking shelter

I run along the alley

tripped by something

I am falling and hitting

the street head on

hard

I get up

and see what

tripped me

a body

lying in the middle of the street

it looks

familiar

still numb and dizzy

I walk over

touching it

turning it over

it's

me

I

turn

I

run

until I find myself back

on cat's avenue

I breath a sigh of relieve

but what a nasty surprise

awaits me

in a torrent of black rain

all I see are the cats

celebrating me

just moments ago

dead or dying

like me

a vision

a fantasy

a dream

an illusion

hallucinations

or just wishfull thinking

by a kitten

imprisoned with its siblings

in a sack

drowning in a river

my love my life

I will give you life

I will hold you

I will feed you

my love my life

I will always be there for you

I will always stand by your side

my love my life

I will guide you

I will follow all your steps

my love my life

I will catch you when you fall

I will pick you up when you lay down face in
dirt

my love my life

I will keep the dream evils at bay while you
sleep

I will drive away the old ghosts scaring you
at night

my love my life

I will give you all

my love my life

but now

I have to let you go

my love my life

fly out

go your own way

choose your own path

choose your own career

maybe becoming a mother yourself

my love my life

breeding the vaccination for love

I have to let go of you

my love

my life

my angel

a past

without a past

a future

without a future

but maybe

a past with a future

and a future

with a past

living in these ageless times

breathing in these timeless ages

we definitely

experience a present

without presence

but what we are

really waiting for

is for the time texting us

*I really don't have time for you guys any
longer*

sorry ;-) ;-)

then we are

really and definitely and absolutely

done for

and our time is

up

rare and precious chain

going back

all the way

how amazing

it is

not just

surviving

world war 1 and 2

not just surviving

the other 30 years of war before

not just surviving

the plague

ideologies

the end of empires

the end of civilizations even

you can go

all the way back

until the beginning of records

you can go

back even further

crossing the wall of written evidence

because

truth to be told

there is still your body

life itself

embodied

inscribed in your body

and this witness

leads all the way back

to the beginning of life

itself

you are just

the last one in a long line

going back

all the way

to the very beginning

you are just

the last in line

you are

the last

in a line

surviving

wars

illnesses

natural distasters

people

believes

culture

art

love

everything there is

out there to kill

you

but

you won't survive

you

the end of the line

ヴァージン・スノー

it snowed

on a rainy day

comforted

I cried

tears of happiness

첫눈

マチネの終わりに

Credits

Written (analogue): 903 and 925, 01.-27.12.2020.

Written (digital): 903, 29.-30.12.2020 and 05.01.2021.

Mix: 903, 31.12.2020 and 05.01.2021.

Writer: j. t. baka.

Photographs: Simon Wagenschütz.

IN MEMORIAM

Impressum

Redaktionsschluss: 21.02.2021.

©2021 baka, j. t.
Herstellung und Verlag: BoD - Books on Demand,
Norderstedt.

ISBN-13: 9783752673166.

MIX

Papier aus ver-
antwortungsvollen
Quellen
Paper from
responsible sources

FSC® C105338